So...

who changed

**Jeffrey
Barlatier**

the
Sabbath?

Printed in the United States of America

9798339276050

Published by Rayna Barlatier Morrisville, North Carolina

Christian Bible Study

Unless otherwise noted, Scripture quotations are from the Holy Bible

TABLE OF CONTENTS

Introduction

The Sabbath has long stood as a cornerstone in the spiritual lives of God's people, stretching back to the very foundation of creation. Yet, the way it's been observed and understood has dramatically shifted over time. To truly grasp the power and meaning of the Sabbath, we've got to take a deep dive into Scripture, where it first appears as a divine rhythm in Genesis and solidifies as a commandment in the Law. From the very beginning, it wasn't just a day off—it was a sacred pause, reflecting God's balance between work and rest.

But here's where it gets interesting: over centuries, this day of rest—originally on the seventh day—underwent serious transformation. What started as a Hebrew tradition rooted in covenant shifted with the rise of Christianity, especially following Jesus' resurrection. Sunday slowly replaced Saturday as the recognized day of worship. But who made that call? Why did it change?

Tracing the evolution of the Sabbath through history, from the early church all the way to modern practice, reveals how social, political, and religious forces all played a part in shaping the Sabbath's identity. It's a story of adaptation, but also of deep theological reasoning. By piecing together, the Scriptural evidence, early church writings, and historical shifts, we can see how this sacred day morphed into what it is today. This exploration forces us to rethink what rest means, how we practice it, and why it's still crucial in a world obsessed with productivity.

What's up with the Sabbath?

The topic of the Sabbath can stir up many emotions and debate. Mention it to anyone, and you'll encounter many theological views among Christians. The Sabbath holds a special place in the heart of God, a divine gift wrapped in rest and reverence. The Sabbath is a foundational concept in biblical theology, deeply embedded in the creation narrative and the covenantal relationship between God and His people. This divine rest establishes the Sabbath as a day of rest, a principle that transcends time and culture, echoing God's rhythm of work and repose.

To study the Sabbath in the Bible is to embark on a journey that reveals God's deepest desire for His people—to dwell in His presence, savor His peace, and reflect His holiness. From the beginning, when God Himself rested on the seventh day, the Sabbath became a symbol of divine love and care, a sacred pause in the rhythm of creation. Throughout Scripture, God calls His people to honor this day, not as a burdensome law, but as an invitation to experience His blessing and restoration. The Sabbath is a covenantal sign, a taste of eternity, where God's people are called to rest in His provision and grace. Digging into the Bible's teachings on the Sabbath uncovers layers of meaning that connect us to the heart of God—His love for us, His desire for our wholeness, and His promise of everlasting rest. The Sabbath is a feast for the soul, a sacred invitation to step away from the hustle of life and savor the richness of rest. Its roots run deep, tracing back to the dawn of creation, where rest wasn't just an option—it was woven into the rhythm of existence. Studying the Sabbath is like uncovering a hidden treasure, offering not only spiritual nourishment but also profound insights into the balance between work and rest, purpose, and peace. As we explore this ancient tradition, we unlock its relevance today, discovering how it can transform our lives by offering restoration, connection, and a deeper sense of meaning.

This book is dedicated to focusing solely on what the Bible says, providing scriptural support for beliefs. It's one thing to follow a belief because someone told you to, but it's quite another to understand and embrace the truth for yourself. This book aims to uncover that truth and clear away any myths and traditions that aren't found in the Bible.

Key Verses:

Matthew 15:52 Then He said to them, "Therefore every scribe instructed concerning the kingdom

of heaven is like a householder who brings out of his treasure things new and old."

1 John 2:6 "whoever says he abides in him ought to walk in the same way in which he walked."

First things first, What the Sabbath isn't

Before diving into what the Sabbath is, let's first discuss what it is not. Misinterpretations of the Sabbath often stem from a lack of understanding of its original purpose, its biblical roots, or its cultural and historical context. Here are some common misunderstandings:

1. Strict Legalism Without Understanding of Purpose:

Some interpretations treat the Sabbath as merely a rigid legal obligation, focusing on the specific restrictions (like not working) while missing the broader purpose of rest, spiritual renewal, and connection with God. This can lead to a burdensome or joyless experience rather than one of peace and reflection.

2. Viewing the Sabbath as Irrelevant Today:

Some people argue that since we are no longer under the Mosaic Law (as taught by some Christian denominations), the Sabbath is obsolete. However, this misses the point that the Sabbath was established long before the Mosaic Law (Genesis 2:2-3) and has spiritual significance beyond the Old Testament legal system. This mindset can be summed up into one word "Antinomianism". Antinomianism is the idea that Christians don't need to follow moral laws because they're saved by grace. This can be risky because it might lead people to justify bad behavior or ignore ethical standards, thinking they don't matter for their faith.

3. *Equating Sunday with the Sabbath:*

In many Christian traditions, Sunday worship has replaced the biblical Sabbath (Saturday). While Sunday is often seen as a day for worship and gathering in honor of Christ's resurrection, some confuse this with the actual Sabbath, which was established on the seventh day in the Bible.

4. Seeing the Sabbath as Just a Day Off:

While rest is a central aspect of the Sabbath, reducing it to merely a break from work without considering the spiritual dimensions (worship, reflection, and gratitude to God) can lead to missing its deeper meaning. It's not just a physical rest day but also a time for spiritual refreshment.

5. Overemphasizing Rules Rather than Relationship:

Focusing only on the rules of Sabbath observance (like which activities are allowed or prohibited) without understanding its intended role in fostering a deeper relationship with God, family, and community can lead to a legalistic and cold interpretation of the day.

6. *Ignoring the Sabbath's Role in Social Justice:*

In the Bible, the Sabbath was also about giving workers and even animals a day of rest (Exodus 20:8-11). It was a form of justice and compassion. Ignoring the Sabbath's implications for labor rights, justice, and human dignity can be a misunderstanding of its broader ethical teachings.

Each of these interpretations misses key aspects of the Sabbath's original purpose: rest, spiritual connection, justice, and renewal.

The Definition of

Sabbath

The word "Sabbath" comes from the Hebrew word *Shabbat*, which means "rest" or "taking a break." It's from the Hebrew verb *shavat*, which is all about stopping or chilling out. The whole idea of the Sabbath shows up early in the Bible, like back in Genesis, when God took a break on the seventh day after creating everything.

The root word *shavat* is tied to the idea of hitting pause—not just on work but on anything going on, whether it's conflict or daily grind. So, at its core, the Sabbath is all about stepping back, reflecting, and keeping things sacred for a day.

History of Sabbath Observance

The history of the Sabbath and its observance is rich and multifaceted, evolving significantly from its origins among the ancient Jews to its influence in America today. Biblical Origins: The Sabbath, or Shabbat, originates in the Hebrew Bible. It is described as a day of rest on the seventh day of the week, commemorating God's rest after creating the world (Genesis 2:2-3). The commandment to observe the Sabbath is given in the Ten Commandments (Exodus 20:8-11 and Deuteronomy 5:12-15).

1.Rabbinic Interpretation:

In ancient Jewish practice, the Sabbath was a day of rest from work and was observed from Friday evening to Saturday evening. Rabbinic literature, including the Mishnah and Talmud, elaborates on the prohibitions and customs associated with the Sabbath. The 39 categories of work forbidden on the Sabbath are detailed in these texts.

2. Early Christianity

Transition to Sunday: Early Christians, many of whom were Jewish, initially observed the Sabbath on Saturday. However, as Christianity developed its identity separate from Judaism, Sunday began to be emphasized as a day of worship in commemoration of Jesus' resurrection. By the 4th century, under Emperor Constantine, Sunday was officially recognized as a day of rest in the Roman Empire.

3. Medieval and Reformation Periods

Medieval Europe: Jewish communities continued to observe the Sabbath in traditional ways, while Christian Europe largely adhered to Sunday observance, with Sunday becoming increasingly institutionalized as a day of rest and church attendance.

Reformation Changes: The Protestant Reformation brought new attitudes towards Sabbath observance. Reformers like Martin Luther and John Calvin advocated for a return to a more scriptural basis, emphasizing the moral importance of Sabbath rest but differing in their practices from the Catholic Church.

4. American Colonial Period:

Puritans and Early Settlers: In Colonial America, particularly in New England, the Sabbath (or Sunday) was strictly observed. Puritans and other religious groups enforced Sabbath laws rigorously, with laws prohibiting work and recreational activities. Sunday was a day for church services, reflection, and rest.

-Diverse Observances: As America became more diverse, Sabbath observance varied. Jewish immigrants continued to observe Shabbat on Saturday, while Christian denominations had different practices regarding Sunday. Over time, religious pluralism led to a range of Sabbath observances and adaptations.

5. Modern America

Secularization and Change: In contemporary America, Sabbath observance has become more flexible. Many people, both religious and secular, do not strictly adhere to traditional practices. The concept of the Sabbath as a day of rest has shifted, with some viewing it more as a personal choice rather than a mandated observance.

Legal and Cultural Aspects: Legal observance of the Sabbath has evolved, particularly with regard to labor laws and business operations. For instance, many businesses remain open on Sundays, reflecting broader cultural shifts. However, laws in some states still recognize Sunday as a day of rest in certain contexts.

Religious Communities: Different religious communities continue to maintain their Sabbath practices. Jewish communities observe Shabbat from Friday evening to Saturday evening, while various Christian denominations observe Sunday in different ways. For some, it remains a day of worship and rest, while others may focus more on personal or family time.

In summary, the Sabbath has transformed significantly from its origins in Jewish tradition to its role in contemporary American society. Its observance reflects a blend of religious, cultural, and societal changes over centuries.

The First Sabbath

The Sabbath wasn't just for Jews or any specific ethnic group; it was established for all of humanity. The concept of the Sabbath is first mentioned in Genesis 2:3, where Moses notes that God rested on the seventh day. This pattern of rest is a consistent theme throughout the Bible.

"Then God blessed the seventh day and sanctified it because on it He ceased from all His work of creation." (NIV)

This passage introduces the Sabbath as a divine institution, establishing a rhythm of work and rest that reflects a fundamental aspect of cosmic order. It embodies a principle of balance and renewal, a concept that resonates deeply with Enlightenment ideals of harmony and natural law.n Genesis 2:2-3, the Sabbath is introduced as a divine institution. God's rest on the seventh day signifies the completion and perfection of creation. The act of resting is not due to any form of exhaustion but is a declaration of the completion and sanctification of the created order. This rest serves as a model for human activity, setting a divine pattern of work and rest. By blessing and sanctifying the seventh day, God establishes it as a holy time, intended for reflection on the goodness and completeness of creation. The Sabbath, therefore, is rooted in the very act of creation and reflects God's rhythm of work and rest.

The Sabbath in Genesis is all about bringing order to the universe. After six days of creating everything, God rests on the seventh day, showing that everything is complete and in balance. It's not just about taking a break—it's about marking the universe as finished and perfectly in sync.

Keyways the Sabbath connects to cosmic order:

1. Completion:

After God finished creating, He rests because the job is done, and everything is in its right place. The Sabbath is a sign that creation has reached a point of order and purpose, nothing more needs to be added.

2. Sacred Time:

By setting aside the seventh day as holy, God creates a rhythm—work for six days, then rest. This pattern mirrors the natural cycles in life and the universe, like day and night, and seasons. It keeps everything in balance.

3. Symbol of Control:

God resting on the seventh day shows His control over creation. It's like saying, "I've got this, the world is in order." This rest isn't just for chilling but symbolizes that everything is running as it should be, under God's watch.

4. Human Connection:

People are invited into this same rhythm. By observing the Sabbath, we're aligning ourselves with the order of the universe. It reminds us that we're part of something bigger, and we're meant to respect that cosmic flow.

In short, the Sabbath in Genesis isn't just about resting—it's about recognizing that the world is perfectly set up and balanced, and we're all a part of that larger order. This passage marks the origin of the Sabbath, highlighting its divine institution. God's rest on the seventh day is not due to fatigue but to signify the completion and perfection of creation.

The Sabbath, therefore, is rooted in creation and reflects a divine order meant to be observed by all.

The Sabbath and the Manna: Exodus 16:23-30

In Exodus 16, we get another look at the Sabbath when the Israelites are in the wilderness. God provides manna for them to eat, but He tells them to collect enough on the sixth day so they don't have to work on the seventh. "This is what the Lord commanded: Tomorrow is to be a day of Sabbath rest, a holy Sabbath to the Lord..." (Exodus 16:23). The message is clear: the Sabbath is about trust. God's got them covered, and they need to rely on Him to provide.

The significance here is that the Sabbath isn't just about stopping work—it's about faith. The Israelites had to trust that God would provide enough for them, even if they took a break. This reflects a larger truth about life: sometimes, we need to step back and trust that things will be okay without our constant input. The Sabbath teaches us to let go of control and recognize that it's God who ultimately sustains us.

Sabbath & Law

Exodus 20:8-11 God outlines the Sabbath in Exodus, emphasizing its sanctity:

"Remember the Sabbath day, to keep it holy. Six days you shall labor, and do all your work, but the seventh day is a Sabbath to the LORD your God. On it, you shall not do any work, you, or your son, or your daughter, your male servant, or your female servant, or your livestock, or the sojourner who is within your gates. For in six days the LORD made heaven and earth, the sea, and all that is in them, and rested on the seventh day. Therefore, the LORD blessed the Sabbath day and made it holy."

Exodus 20:8-11, which contains the Fourth Commandment, introduces the Sabbath into the law for the Israelites. This commandment is about keeping the seventh day holy and is grounded in the idea of rest and divine order. Here's a breakdown of its meaning and significance:

1. Command to Rest

- "Remember the Sabbath day by keeping it holy" (Exodus 20:8)

The commandment opens by telling the Israelites to "remember" the Sabbath, meaning it was already established (as in Genesis) and should be honored. To "keep it holy" means to set it apart from the rest of the week. It's a day dedicated to God, not just a regular day off.

2. Six Days of Work, One Day of Rest

- "Six days you shall labor and do all your work, but the seventh day is a sabbath to the Lord your God. On it, you shall not do any work..." (Exodus 20:9-10):

The structure of the commandment creates a rhythm—work for six days, rest on the seventh. This cycle is tied to productivity and rest but also signals a balance in life. The idea is that work is important, but so is stopping to recharge and reflect. The rest applies to everyone: adults, children, servants, even animals. It's a universal principle, showing the importance of rest for all of creation.

3. Grounded in Creation

- For in six days the Lord made the heavens and the earth... but He rested on the seventh day. Therefore, the Lord blessed the Sabbath day and made it holy" (Exodus 20:11)

This section connects the Sabbath command to the creation story in Genesis, where God rested on the seventh day after creating the world. The idea is that humans should imitate God's work-rest pattern. It's not just about physical rest, but also about reflecting on the order and purpose of life, mirroring God's example of resting after establishing the cosmos.

4. Spiritual and Social Implications

- The Sabbath is more than a rule about time off; it's a covenant between God and His people. It reflects God's authority over time and creation, and by observing it, the Israelites acknowledge that God is in control.

- Socially, it's also a statement of equality and justice. The commandment ensures that everyone, regardless of status, gets a day of rest. This was particularly important in a society where servants and workers might otherwise be exploited.

5. Symbol of Freedom and Trust

- By resting, the Israelites are reminded that their lives and work depend on God, not just their own efforts. It requires faith to stop working, trusting that God will provide. It's also a reminder of their freedom from slavery in Egypt, where they couldn't rest. Now, under God's law, rest becomes a symbol of liberation and trust.

The Sabbath law in Exodus 20 highlights a deeper principle of balance, rest, and divine order. It's not just a command to take a day off but an acknowledgment of God's sovereignty, a reflection of creation, and a statement of social justice. It shapes how the Israelites understand time, work, and their relationship with God and each other. The commandment to observe the Sabbath, extending to all including servants and animals.

The Sabbath Sign

Exodus 31:15-17- Exodus 31:15 (NIV): "For six days, work is to be done, but the seventh day is a day of sabbath rest, holy to the Lord. Whoever does any work on the Sabbath day is to be put to death."

- Exodus 31:16 (NIV): "The Israelites are to observe the Sabbath, celebrating it for the generations to come as a lasting covenant."

- Exodus 31:17 (NIV): "It will be a sign between me and the Israelites forever, for in six days the Lord made the heavens and the earth, and on the seventh day he rested and was refreshed.":

1. *Work and Rest Cycle (Verse 15) Six Days of Work*: The command emphasizes a balanced rhythm of labor and rest. The six-day work period

underscores the importance of productive work as part of life, while also setting a clear boundary for rest.

- Sabbath Rest: The seventh day is designated as a "sabbath rest" and is "holy to the Lord." This distinction highlights the Sabbath as a special, consecrated time set apart from regular work and activities.

- Penalty for Violation: The severe penalty for working on the Sabbath (death) underscores the command's importance and the need for communal respect for divine laws. This reflects the seriousness with which the Sabbath is to be observed, ensuring that its sanctity is maintained.

2. Enduring Covenant (Verse 16):

- Observance and Celebration: The Sabbath is to be "observed" and "celebrated" throughout generations, emphasizing its ongoing relevance and importance in the life of the community. It's more than a rule; it's a tradition to be cherished and honored.

- Lasting Covenant: Calling it a "lasting covenant" indicates that the Sabbath is an enduring part of the divine agreement between God and the Israelites. This is not a temporary command but a perpetual aspect of their spiritual and communal identity.

3. Sign of the Covenant and Creation (Verse 17):

- Sign Between God and the Israelite: The Sabbath serves as a tangible symbol of the special relationship between God and His people. It is a marker of their covenantal bond and a sign of their unique identity as God's chosen people.

- Connection to Creation: By referencing God's rest on the seventh day, the verse ties the Sabbath to

the creation narrative. It underscores that the Sabbath is rooted in the divine order established at the beginning of time, reinforcing its foundational role in the created world.

- *God's Rest and Refreshment:* The mention of God being "refreshed" (or "ceased from work") on the seventh day highlights that the Sabbath represents a divine pattern of rest and completion. It's not just about physical rest but about recognizing the completion and perfection of God's creation.

Exodus 31:15-17 highlights the Sabbath as a divinely ordained period of rest, deeply rooted in creation and established as a lasting covenant between God and the Israelites. It sets a clear work-rest cycle, mandates severe penalties for its violation to ensure its sanctity and serves as a perpetual sign of the covenant. The Sabbath's connection to God's rest reinforces its importance as a fundamental and sacred practice in the life of the community.

The Sabbath and the Manna: Exodus 16:23-30

In Exodus 16, we get another look at the Sabbath when the Israelites are in the wilderness. God provides manna for them to eat, but He tells them to collect enough on the sixth day so they don't have to work on the seventh. "This is what the Lord commanded: Tomorrow is to be a day of Sabbath rest, a holy Sabbath to the Lord..." (Exodus 16:23). The message is clear: the Sabbath is about trust. God's got them covered, and they need to rely on Him to provide.

The significance here is that the Sabbath isn't just about stopping work—it's about faith. The

Israelites had to trust that God would provide enough for them, even if they took a break. This reflects a larger truth about life: sometimes, we need to step back and trust that things will be okay without our constant input. The Sabbath teaches us to let go of control and recognize that it's God who ultimately sustains us.

The Sabbath and Worship: Leviticus 23:3

In Leviticus, the Sabbath is also tied to worship: "There are six days when you may work, but the seventh day is a day of Sabbath rest, a day of sacred assembly..." (Leviticus 23:3). This verse highlights the communal aspect of the Sabbath—it's not just about personal rest, but about gathering together to worship God.

The Sabbath here becomes a day not only for physical rest but for spiritual community. It's a time to come together, reflect on God's goodness, and participate in collective worship. In today's fast-paced, individualistic society, this idea of shared rest and worship feels more necessary than ever. The Sabbath is a reminder that we're not meant to go through life alone—we're meant to connect with each other and with God.

The Sabbath and Liberation: Deuteronomy 5:12-15

In Deuteronomy, Moses retells the Ten Commandments, but this time the Sabbath is linked to Israel's liberation from Egypt: "Remember that you were slaves in Egypt and that the Lord your God brought you out of there..." (Deuteronomy

5:15). The Sabbath is a reminder of freedom—it's a symbol of the fact that God rescued them from a life of forced labor.

By tying the Sabbath to freedom from slavery, this passage shows that the Sabbath is about liberation, not just from work but from the constant pressures of life. It's a day to step away from everything that enslaves us—whether it's our jobs, our worries, or our need to constantly produce—and reconnect with the freedom that comes from God. It's about reclaiming our time and our identity as people who are more than what we do for a living.

The Spirit of the Sabbath: Isaiah 58:13-14

Isaiah brings the focus to the heart of the Sabbath: "If you call the Sabbath a delight and the Lord's holy day honorable... then you will find your joy in the Lord..." (Isaiah 58:13-14). This passage emphasizes that the Sabbath is not just a rule to follow but something to be enjoyed. It's about finding joy in the presence of God and celebrating the holiness of the day.

This passage strips away the legalism and shows that the Sabbath is meant to be a blessing. It's not just about doing nothing; it's about finding joy, refreshment, and deeper connection with God. When we embrace the Sabbath as a gift rather than a burden, it transforms the way we experience rest and worship.

Severity of Sabbath

Punishment

Numbers 15:32-36 tells a story where a guy was caught collecting wood on the Sabbath, which was a big no-no. The punishment for this violation was extreme—he was stoned to death. This story highlights just how seriously the Sabbath was taken in ancient Israel.

Here's the modern take: The Sabbath was more than just a day off; it was a crucial part of the community's relationship with God. Violating it was seen as a major offense. The severe punishment shows that keeping the Sabbath was about maintaining respect for God's rules and ensuring that everyone in the community followed them.

The passage also reflects on the community's role in enforcing religious laws. By punishing the offender, the community was upholding its collective commitment to divine commands and keeping itself spiritually pure. The execution outside the camp symbolized removing wrongdoing from the group, keeping the community focused on its religious commitments.

Lastly, this story brings up important questions about balancing strict adherence to rules with compassion. While the punishment was harsh, it raised discussions on how to apply religious laws fairly and ethically in practice.

So, in a nutshell, Numbers 15:32-36 shows us the high stakes of Sabbath observance, the importance of community enforcement, and the ongoing discussion about balancing justice with mercy.

Jeremiah 17:21-27 – The Sabbath as a Litmus Test for Faithfulness

In Jeremiah 17:21-27, God speaks through the prophet, calling on the people of Judah to "be careful not to carry a load on the Sabbath day or bring it through the gates of Jerusalem." The instruction is clear—no work should be done on the Sabbath, and the people must keep it holy. The warning follows: "If you do not obey... I will kindle an unquenchable fire in the gates of Jerusalem that will consume her fortresses" (Jer. 17:27, NIV).

For Jeremiah, the Sabbath wasn't just about following the rules; it was a sign of the people's obedience to God. The act of carrying loads into the city may seem minor, but it symbolized a deeper issue—a disregard for divine instruction. Walter Brueggemann, in *Sabbath as Resistance*, highlights that the Sabbath, in its purest form, is a rejection of the "culture of now," which prioritizes work and consumption over spiritual health (Brueggemann, 2014). By neglecting the Sabbath, the people of Judah were effectively rejecting God's provision and attempting to control their own destinies. Jeremiah's message is that when people forget to rest and trust in God's sovereignty, they invite chaos—hence the image of Jerusalem being consumed by fire.

In our modern context, the constant push to always be productive mirrors Judah's struggle. The message is clear: refusing to rest, and instead always striving to do more, carries both personal and communal consequences. The Sabbath is a moment to realign with God, acknowledging that we are not defined by our output.

Isaiah 56:2-7 – The Sabbath as an Invitation to Outsiders

Isaiah 56 takes the concept of the Sabbath to another level by widening its scope. God, through Isaiah, tells the people: "Blessed is the one who... keeps the Sabbath without desecrating it, and keeps their hands from doing any evil" (Isa. 56:2, NIV). But Isaiah doesn't stop there. He goes on to say that even foreigners and eunuchs—those traditionally excluded from Israel's religious community—are welcome if they observe the Sabbath. The text reads, "To the eunuchs who keep my Sabbaths... I will give within my temple and its walls a memorial and a name better than sons and daughters" (Isa. 56:4-5, NIV).

Isaiah shifts the conversation from mere rule-following to inclusivity. The Sabbath becomes not just an obligation for the Israelites but an open door for all people. Abraham Joshua Heschel, in his work *The Sabbath*, emphasizes that the Sabbath is not just a Jewish institution but a "cathedral in time" where all who seek God can find peace and connection (Heschel, 2005). Isaiah's vision is radical because it breaks down social and religious barriers—foreigners and eunuchs, who were often marginalized, are given the same standing as Israelites if they honor the Sabbath.

In today's urban, multicultural world, Isaiah's message is especially relevant. Observing the Sabbath, in this sense, becomes not just about personal rest but about creating a community where everyone can experience God's presence. The inclusion of "outsiders" resonates in a society that still grapples with issues of exclusion and belonging.

Isaiah 58:13-14 – The Sabbath as a Source of Joy

Isaiah 58:13-14 brings a more personal and intimate take on the Sabbath, urging people to "call the Sabbath a delight and the Lord's holy day honorable." It goes further, saying, "if you honor it by not going your own way... then you will find your joy in the Lord" (Isa. 58:13-14, NIV).

Isaiah flips the script here by shifting the focus from obligation to joy. The Sabbath isn't meant to feel like a burden; it's supposed to be a time where people experience deep, authentic joy in the Lord. Heschel talks about the Sabbath as a time to "mend" our relationship with God, a moment where we stop working to rediscover what truly matters (Heschel, 2005). In Isaiah's view, the Sabbath isn't just a rule to follow; it's a gift—a divine opportunity to rest in God's provision and find peace that transcends the busyness of life.

In urban culture today, where "the grind" is celebrated, Isaiah's message is countercultural. To "delight" in rest is almost revolutionary, especially when the world around us prizes productivity above all else. Isaiah reminds us that the Sabbath isn't just about stopping work—it's about finding joy in that pause, a joy that only comes from spiritual fulfillment.

Did Jesus Flip the Script (make a change) to the Sabbath?

Jesus didn't come to flip the script on the Sabbath; rather, He aimed to give it more depth and meaning. His approach wasn't about ditching or changing the Sabbath, but about fulfilling its true purpose and intent.

In Matthew 5:17-18 Jesus makes it clear: "Do not think that I have come to abolish the Law or the Prophets; I have not come to abolish them but to fulfill them." He's not here to erase the old rules but to bring out their full meaning. This shows that Jesus respected the Sabbath and saw it as part of a bigger picture rather than something to be discarded.

Luke 4:16 shows that Jesus followed Sabbath traditions, going to the synagogue on the Sabbath day just as He was expected to. This wasn't about changing the rules but honoring them, reflecting His commitment to the practices of His time.

In Mark 2:27 Jesus redefines the Sabbath by saying, "The Sabbath was made for man, not man for the Sabbath." He's highlighting that the Sabbath is meant to serve humanity, not the other way around. It's about using the day to benefit people, not just to follow rules.

Jesus also pointed out in Matthew 12:12 that "it is lawful to do good on the Sabbath." By doing good, like healing and helping others, you're aligning with what the Sabbath is supposed to be about. It's a day for compassion and kindness, not just for rigid rule-following.

So, in essence, Jesus wasn't here to scrap the Sabbath but to refresh its purpose. He clarified that it's meant for human benefit and mercy, aligning

with a deeper understanding rather than just sticking

to outdated rules.

Jesus' Approach to

the Sabbath

Jesus' understanding of the Sabbath was revolutionary, shifting it from a rigid, legalistic practice to a compassionate and life-giving principle. In His time, religious leaders, particularly the Pharisees, had turned the Sabbath into a set of strict rules that weighed people down. Jesus, however, saw the Sabbath in a much deeper and more human-centered way, emphasizing mercy, rest, and restoration over rigid observance.

-The Sabbath Was Made for Humanity

One of Jesus' most famous statements about the Sabbath is found in Mark 2:27: "The Sabbath was made for man, not man for the Sabbath." This flips the script on how people viewed the day of rest. Jesus wanted to show that the Sabbath wasn't meant to be a burden; it was a gift for humanity. It was a day designed for people to step away from the grind of everyday life, reconnect with themselves, others, and God. In today's fast-paced world, that kind of rest is something we desperately need. Jesus highlighted that the Sabbath should serve us, not the other way around, giving people a chance to recharge mentally, physically, and spiritually.

-Compassion Over Legalism

Throughout His ministry, Jesus clashed with the Pharisees over how to observe the Sabbath. They had a long list of things that people couldn't do on that day, including healing the sick. But Jesus made it clear that showing compassion—helping someone in need—was at the heart of the Sabbath. In Matthew 12:12, He says, "It is lawful to do good on the Sabbath." Jesus wasn't interested in following rules just for the sake of it. His focus was on restoring people and showing mercy.

By healing people on the Sabbath (as in Matthew 12:9-13 and Luke 13:10-17), Jesus emphasized that the day should be life-affirming. For Him, it was all about doing good, caring for others, and ensuring that the Sabbath was a time of joy and restoration, not restriction. His approach speaks to us today, reminding us that the day of rest should never be about following rules blindly but about caring for ourselves and others.

-Lord of the Sabbath

Jesus didn't just reinterpret the Sabbath—He made it clear that He had authority over it. In Mark 2:28, He says, "The Son of Man is Lord even of the Sabbath." This was a bold statement, especially in a society where the Sabbath was one of the most sacred commandments. But what Jesus was saying is that the Sabbath was ultimately about Him. The rest and restoration that the Sabbath symbolizes are fully realized in the peace and wholeness that Jesus offers.

He wasn't doing away with the Sabbath; He was showing that it points to something greater—a deeper rest found in Him. In declaring Himself "Lord of the Sabbath," Jesus showed that He is the source of true rest and that honoring the Sabbath goes beyond simply observing a day. It's about finding peace in Him.

-Sabbath as a Time for Restoration

Jesus saw the Sabbath as more than just physical rest; it was about restoring people to wholeness. When He healed on the Sabbath, like the woman with a disabling spirit in Luke 13:10-17,

He was making a point. The Sabbath is about freedom—freedom from what holds us back, whether it's illness, stress, or burdens. Jesus used the day of rest to show what it means to be restored, to be set free. This speaks to the idea that rest isn't just about stopping work; it's about finding healing and wholeness in all aspects of life.

-A Deeper Spiritual Rest

Jesus also pointed to the fact that the Sabbath wasn't just about a single day but about a deeper, ongoing spiritual rest. In Matthew 11:28, He says, "Come to me, all who labor and are heavy laden, and I will give you rest." He offers a kind of rest that transcends the physical. It's the rest we find when we let go of our anxieties, when we trust God, and when we allow ourselves to be at peace. Jesus' message was that, ultimately, the Sabbath points to this deeper rest, a peace that comes from knowing we don't have to strive all the time. It's the rest found in God's presence.

Jesus' understanding of the Sabbath wasn't about following strict rules; it was about compassion, restoration, and a deeper, spiritual rest. He took the day of rest and gave it new meaning, showing that it should serve humanity, not burden it. By healing on the Sabbath and declaring Himself "Lord of the Sabbath," Jesus redefined the day as one of mercy, renewal, and reflection. In today's world, where the lines between work and rest are often blurred, His message is more relevant than ever. The Sabbath isn't just a day off—it's a chance to reconnect with what truly matters and to find peace in Him.

Early Christian

Practices

The way early Christians observed the Sabbath evolved significantly as their faith transitioned from its Jewish roots to a broader Christian identity. Initially, many of the first followers of Christ were Jewish, and they continued to observe the Sabbath on Saturday, following the commandments outlined in the Mosaic law. But as Christianity spread and new believers, especially non-Jews, came into the faith, the practices around Sabbath-keeping began to shift, blending tradition with the new realities of the Christian message.

-Early Jewish-Christian Sabbath Practices

In the early days, Jewish Christians kept the Sabbath on Saturday, just as they had before becoming followers of Christ. The Sabbath, rooted in the creation story and the Ten Commandments, was a key part of Jewish identity and religious life. For them, this meant gathering in synagogues for prayer, reading the scriptures, and honoring the command to rest on the seventh day.

But for these Jewish Christians, there was already a shift happening. Jesus had redefined the Sabbath as a day not just for rest but for doing good. He showed that the Sabbath was about more than just following rules—it was about compassion, mercy, and connecting with God in meaningful ways. This understanding influenced how early Jewish Christians viewed the Sabbath, making it less about strict observance and more about embodying the spirit of rest and renewal that the day was meant to bring.

-The Rise of Sunday Worship

As Christianity spread beyond its Jewish origins, especially into Gentile (non-Jewish) communities, the practice of gathering on Sunday began to gain significance. By the second century, many Christians were meeting on Sunday, which they called "the Lord's Day" (based on Revelation 1:10), in honor of Jesus' resurrection, which had taken place on a Sunday. This day quickly became central to Christian worship, symbolizing the new life that Christ brought through His resurrection.

Sunday gatherings weren't just about rest—they were about celebrating the core of Christian faith: Jesus' victory over death. Early Christians would meet to break bread (in the form of the Eucharist or communion), pray, and study the scriptures together. While the traditional Sabbath was still important, Sunday became the day that defined Christian community and worship.

-The Transition Period: Dual Observance

During the early years of the church, many believers observed both the Jewish Sabbath on Saturday and the Lord's Day on Sunday. This dual observance reflected the blending of old traditions with new faith. They would rest and reflect on the Sabbath in line with Jewish customs, and then on Sunday, they'd gather to celebrate Jesus' resurrection with fellow believers.

Over time, as Christianity grew and became more distinct from Judaism, Sunday gradually took precedence. It became less about resting on the seventh day and more about honoring Christ through worship, fellowship, and celebration of His resurrection. The emphasis moved from simply following a law to engaging in a deeper, spiritual rest and renewal that pointed to the ultimate rest found in Jesus.

The way early Christians observed the Sabbath shows how their practices were deeply influenced by their Jewish roots but evolved as their understanding of Jesus grew. While the traditional Saturday Sabbath remained a part of their lives for a time, Sunday, the day of resurrection, became the focal point of Christian worship. This shift represents more than just a change in schedule—it reflects how early Christians reinterpreted rest, worship, and community life in light of Jesus' teachings and the new hope He brought to the world.

Were the Apostles

Team Sabbath?

The early apostles did indeed observe the Sabbath, reflecting their roots in Jewish tradition and culture. This practice is evident in several key moments from the New Testament.

For instance, Paul and Barnabas adhered to Sabbath observance during their missions. In Acts 13:14, they went to the synagogue on the Sabbath in Antioch to preach, indicating that they saw the Sabbath as an opportunity to connect with Jewish audiences. Similarly, in Acts 17:2, Paul frequented the synagogue in Thessalonica on the Sabbath, and in Acts 18:4, he continued to do so in Corinth. These instances show that observing the Sabbath was part of their routine and mission strategy.

In the early church, the apostles' observance of the Sabbath was in line with their Jewish heritage.

This was not just a ritual but a practical means of teaching and engaging with Jewish communities. However, as the church began to establish its own identity, a shift occurred. Early Christians started to gather on Sunday, the first day of the week, to celebrate Jesus' resurrection. This change is recorded in Acts 20:7, where the disciples came together on Sunday to break bread.

In summary, while the early apostles initially observed the Sabbath as part of their Jewish practices, the growing Christian community gradually transitioned to Sunday worship. This shift reflects the evolution of early Christian identity while maintaining respect for the Sabbath's significance.

The Shift from Saturday Sabbath to Sunday Worship

The transition from Saturday Sabbath observance to Sunday worship within the Catholic Church is a significant theological and historical shift, shaped by centuries of evolving Christian practice. This change was not merely a simple alteration of the day of rest but reflected a profound transformation in understanding Christian worship and the nature of the Sabbath.

One of the earliest formal declarations of this transition occurred at the Council of Laodicea, convened around 363-364 AD. Canon 29 of the council explicitly states, "Christians must not Judaize by resting on the Sabbath, but must work on that day, honoring the Lord's Day; and, if they can, resting then as Christians. But if any shall be found to be Judaizers, let them be anathema from

Christ" (*Council of Laodicea*, Canon 29). This canon marks a decisive move away from Saturday Sabbath observance, establishing Sunday as the primary day for Christian worship and rest.

The significance of this shift is further elaborated in the *Catechism of the Catholic Church*. Paragraph 2175 notes, "The Church celebrates the day of Christ's Resurrection on the 'eighth day,' which is Sunday: 'We all gather on the day of the sun because it is the first day, the day of Christ's resurrection'" (*Catechism of the Catholic Church*, Paragraph 2175). This passage underscores Sunday's role as the principal day for Christian gatherings, emphasizing its connection to the resurrection of Jesus, which is central to Christian faith.

The theological importance of Sunday was reinforced in Pope John Paul II's Apostolic Letter *Dies Domini* (1998), which affirms, "The Sunday celebration of the Lord's Day and his Eucharist is at the heart of the Church's life. It is the day on which the Paschal Mystery is celebrated in the Eucharist and the faithful are called to participate in the solemn liturgical celebration of Christ's resurrection" (*Dies Domini*, Paragraph 66). This letter reaffirms Sunday's central role in Catholic worship, highlighting its significance in celebrating Christ's resurrection and the new creation.

In summary, the shift from Saturday to Sunday worship within the Catholic Church was a gradual process influenced by theological reflection and practical considerations. This transition was formalized through various councils and documents, which emphasized the resurrection of Jesus as the focal point of Christian worship. The shift reflects a deeper understanding of the Sabbath's purpose, moving from a strict adherence to the old covenant to embracing the new covenant established through Christ.

So, What Now?

The question of whether Christians should observe the Sabbath on Saturday, Sunday, or both reflects a complex interplay of historical practices and theological developments. The answer varies based on denominational beliefs, historical contexts, and personal convictions.

Historically, the Sabbath was observed on Saturday, the seventh day of the week, as prescribed in the Old Testament. This day of rest was rooted in the creation narrative, where God rested on the seventh day (Genesis 2:2-3), and later codified in the Mosaic Law (Exodus 20:8-11). For many Jewish communities and some Christian groups, Saturday remains the Sabbath, a day dedicated to rest and worship.

Early Christians, following the resurrection of Jesus, began to shift their observance to Sunday, the first day of the week, as highlighted in the New Testament (Acts 20:7; 1 Corinthians 16:2). This transition was further solidified by Emperor Constantine's Edict of 321 AD, which established Sunday as a day of rest throughout the Roman Empire.

For many contemporary Christians, Sunday observance is seen as a fulfillment of the Sabbath rather than a replacement. They view the shift as a movement from the old covenant to the new covenant in Christ, celebrating the resurrection and new life offered through Jesus. This perspective aligns with themes of grace and renewal rather than a strict adherence to Old Testament Sabbath laws.

Conversely, denominations such as the Seventh-day Adventists continue to observe the Sabbath on Saturday, maintaining a commitment to the Fourth Commandment's call for rest on the seventh day. They argue that the commandment remains valid and binding.

Christian practices around Sabbath observance reflect a range of theological beliefs and historical influences, illustrating the diverse ways in which the Sabbath has been understood and practiced across different contexts.:

Saturday Observance

For some Christian groups, the Sabbath is observed on Saturday. Seventh-day Adventists, for instance, take their Sabbath seriously from Friday evening to Saturday evening. They follow this practice based on the Fourth Commandment and the creation story, using this time for rest, worship, and reflection. Seventh Day Baptists also honor the Sabbath on Saturday, echoing a similar commitment to the biblical command.

Messianic Jews, who blend Jewish traditions with belief in Jesus as the Messiah, also celebrate the Sabbath on Saturday. Their observance aligns with traditional Jewish customs, maintaining the ancient practices that define their faith.

Sunday Observance

In contrast, the majority of Christian denominations around the world observe Sunday as their primary day of worship. The Roman Catholic Church, for example, marks Sunday to commemorate the resurrection of Jesus. This shift from Saturday to Sunday as a day of worship began early in Christian history and was solidified by the Catholic Church.

Eastern Orthodox Christians follow a similar practice, celebrating Sunday as a day of resurrection and worship. This tradition reflects the early Christian move away from the Jewish Sabbath to a focus on Christ's resurrection. Most Protestant denominations, including Baptists, Methodists, and Lutherans, also observe. This practice aligns with the broader Christian emphasis on celebrating the resurrection and signifies a transition from Jewish customs.

Anglicans and Episcopalians are on the same page, celebrating Sunday as the Lord's Day. Their practice is in line with early Christian traditions and reinforces the importance of Sunday in Christian worship.

Globally, while Sunday is the main day of worship for most Christian denominations, there are notable exceptions like the Seventh-day Adventists and Seventh Day Baptists who stick with Saturday. This diversity in observance highlights the rich tapestry of Christian practice and belief, showing how historical and theological factors shape how people honor the Sabbath.

Many Christians reconcile these different observances by focusing on the underlying principle of Sabbath rest and worship. Whether observing Saturday or Sunday, the emphasis is often on the spiritual significance of dedicating time to rest, reflection, and relationship with God. The day chosen for this purpose becomes less about the specific day itself and more about honoring the spirit of rest and renewal.

In essence, whether Christians observe the Sabbath on Saturday, Sunday, or both, the key is understanding the underlying principles of rest, worship, and connection with God. This flexibility allows for a range of practices that reflect personal, denominational, and historical contexts while emphasizing the shared goal of spiritual enrichment and community.

A Christian who observes both Saturday and Sunday as days of rest and worship is often referred to as a "Sabbatarian "practicing" "dual observance." This approach reflects a commitment to honoring the Sabbath tradition from both Jewish and Christian perspectives.

The term "Sabbatarian" generally denotes someone who adheres to the practice of keeping the Sabbath day holy. Traditionally, this refers to

Saturday, the Jewish Sabbath, which has deep roots in biblical law and history. In contrast, Sunday observance is rooted in Christian tradition, commemorating the resurrection of Jesus and representing the "Lord's Day."

Practicing dual observance involves recognizing the significance of both days. By doing so, individuals aim to honor the historical and theological importance of the Saturday Sabbath while also celebrating the Sunday resurrection. This approach integrates elements from both traditions, showing respect for the Jewish origins of the Sabbath and the Christian reinterpretation of Sunday as a day of worship.

In essence, a Christian who observes both days is blending these rich traditions, reflecting a broader and inclusive view of Sabbath observance that respects both the Old Testament roots and the

new covenant established through Jesus.

What about the Sabbath in the Epistle of Hebrews?

The Epistle to the Hebrews provides a nuanced understanding of the Sabbath, focusing on its theological implications rather than its traditional observance. The key passages related to the Sabbath in Hebrews offer insights into how the early Christian community interpreted this day in light of the new covenant established through Jesus Christ.:

Hebrews 4:1-11: This passage is central to understanding the Sabbath in Hebrews. The author of Hebrews discusses a "Sabbath rest" that remains for the people of God. The text states:

Hebrews 4:9-10: "There remains, then, a Sabbath-rest for the people of God; for anyone who enters God's rest also rests from their works, just as God did from his."

-The "rest" referred to here is not limited to a particular day but represents a spiritual state of rest in Christ. This passage connects the concept of Sabbath rest to the broader theme of entering God's rest through faith in Jesus. It emphasizes that Jesus, as the high priest, offers a superior rest compared to the Old Testament Sabbath.

Theological Implications

-Fulfillment in Christ: The writer of Hebrews argues that Jesus fulfills the promise of Sabbath rest. In the Old Testament, the Sabbath was a day of physical rest, but in the New Testament understanding, it symbolizes a deeper spiritual rest that comes from salvation through Christ.

- Rest from Works: The passage contrasts the rest of faith in Christ with the Old Testament Sabbath, which was observed as a day of cessation from labor. The new Sabbath rest is about ceasing from self-reliant efforts to achieve righteousness and resting in the completed work of Christ.

3. *Typology and Fulfillment:*

- Hebrews 4:1: "Therefore, since the promise of entering his rest still stands, let us be careful that none of you be found to have fallen short of it."

- This verse highlights that the promise of rest is still available through Christ, suggesting that the physical observance of the Sabbath is a type or shadow of the spiritual reality found in Christ. The emphasis is on the fulfillment of the Sabbath rest in Jesus, not merely the observance of a specific day.

In Hebrews, the Sabbath is reinterpreted as a symbol of the spiritual rest that believers find in Christ. The physical observance of the Sabbath is seen as a precursor to the deeper rest provided by

Jesus' redemptive work. Rather than focusing on a particular day, the Epistle to the Hebrews emphasizes entering God's rest through faith in Jesus, marking a transition from Old Testament practices to the new covenant.

When we look at the Sabbath across the Bible, it's clear that its meaning has evolved from the Old Testament to the New Testament. In the Old Testament, the Sabbath is a day set aside for rest and worship, a divine command that reflects God's rest after creation. It's a day to step back, refresh, and focus on spiritual renewal.

Fast forward to the New Testament, and Jesus and the Epistle to the Hebrews take this concept further. Jesus highlights that the Sabbath was meant to benefit people, not just be a strict rule to follow. He brings a new perspective that the true rest of the Sabbath is found in Him. The Epistle to the Hebrews picks up on this idea, suggesting that the Sabbath's deeper meaning is fulfilled through faith in Christ, representing a spiritual rest rather than just a physical day of rest.

Jesus & the Sabbath

Jesus and the Sabbath share several key similarities, reflecting their deep connection within the Christian faith. Here's a simplified look at how they align:

1. *Purpose of Rest and Renewal*

-Sabbath: Established as a day of rest (Exodus 20:8-11). It's a time to pause from work and focus on spiritual renewal and connection with God.

- Jesus: Offers spiritual rest and renewal (Matthew 11:28). He invites people to come to Him for rest and relief from life's burdens.

2. *Fulfillment of Divine Promise*

- Sabbath: A divine institution reflecting God's completed work in creation (Genesis 2:2-3). It symbolizes divine rest and completeness.

- Jesus: Fulfilled the Law and prophets, including the Sabbath (Matthew 5:17). He represents the ultimate rest and completion of God's promises through His work on the cross and resurrection.

3. The Symbol of Holiness

- Sabbath: Declared holy by God (Exodus 20:8). It's a day set apart from the ordinary for spiritual purposes.

- Jesus: Embodies divine holiness (John 1:14). His life and teachings set apart a new way of understanding and living out God's holiness.

4. *Source of Healing and Restoration*

- Sabbath: Associated with healing and restoration in the Old Testament (Isaiah 58:13-14). It's a time for physical and spiritual rejuvenation.

- Jesus: Heals on the Sabbath and emphasizes its true purpose (Mark 3:1-6). His actions underscore that the Sabbath is for doing good and bringing healing.

5. New Covenant and Transformation

- Sabbath: Represents the old covenant's sign of rest and relationship with God (Exodus 31:16-17).

- Jesus: Brings a new covenant, transforming the understanding of rest and worship (Luke 22:20). He shifts the focus from legalistic observance to a relationship-based approach.

6. Central Role in Worship

- Sabbath: Central to Jewish worship and spiritual rhythm.

- Jesus: Central to Christian worship, being the focus of Sunday observance as the day of His resurrection (Acts 20:7; 1 Corinthians 16:2).

In essence, Jesus and the Sabbath are intertwined through their roles in providing spiritual rest, fulfilling divine promises, embodying holiness, offering healing, and marking a transformative shift in religious practice. While the Sabbath was a day set aside for rest and renewal in the old covenant, Jesus brings a deeper, more personal experience of rest and spiritual fulfillment in the new covenant.

The Apostle to the

Gentiles

Paul's verse in Colossians 2:16-17 is often discussed in relation to the Sabbath and its observance in the Christian context. The passage reads:

"Therefore, do not let anyone judge you by what you eat or drink, or with regard to a religious festival, a New Moon celebration or a Sabbath day. These are a shadow of the things that were to come; the reality, however, is found in Christ."* (Colossians 2:16-17, NIV)

In Colossians 2, Paul addresses concerns about legalism and asceticism that were affecting the early Christian community. Some teachers were insisting that adherence to Jewish laws and customs, including dietary restrictions and observance of religious festivals, was necessary for spiritual growth. Paul counters this by emphasizing that these practices were shadows pointing to the reality found in Christ.

Theological Implications

Paul's reference to the Sabbath in this passage signifies a shift from the old covenant practices to the new covenant established by Christ. By saying that "the reality, however, is found in Christ," Paul underscores that the Sabbath, along with other Old Testament rituals, was a foreshadowing of the ultimate fulfillment found in Jesus. The Sabbath, while a meaningful observance in the Jewish tradition, is seen as part of the broader set of Old Testament practices that pointed forward to the coming of Christ.

Impact on Sabbath Observance

Paul's teaching suggests that Christian believers are no longer bound by the ceremonial laws and observances of the Old Testament, including the Sabbath. This does not mean the Sabbath loses its significance, but rather that its role changes in light of Christ's redemptive work. For Christians, the focus shifts from strict adherence to Sabbath laws to living in the freedom and rest provided by Christ.

What are Types and Shadows? A Broader Christian Understanding

This perspective helps explain why early Christians transitioned from observing the Sabbath on Saturday to celebrating Sunday as the Lord's Day. The celebration of Sunday, the day of Christ's resurrection, is viewed as a fulfillment of the Sabbath rest, embodying the spiritual rest and renewal offered through Jesus. The shift reflects an understanding that while the Sabbath was a shadow, Christ represents the substance and reality that it pointed toward.

The concept of "types and shadows" refers to Old Testament practices, events, and symbols that prefigure and find their ultimate fulfillment in the New Testament through Jesus Christ. These types and shadows provide a richer understanding of how the Old Testament anticipates the new covenant established in the New Testament. Here are some key examples:

1.   The Passover Lamb

Old Testament Type: The Passover lamb was a central symbol in the Exodus narrative. In Exodus 12, the Israelites were instructed to sacrifice a lamb and smear its blood on their doorposts so that the angel of death would pass over their homes during the final plague on Egypt. This act of sacrifice and the subsequent deliverance from death and slavery prefigured a greater redemption.

New Testament Fulfillment: Jesus is identified as the ultimate Passover Lamb in John 1:29, where John the Baptist declares, "Look, the Lamb of God, who takes away the sin of the world!" Jesus' sacrificial death on the cross and His resurrection provide a complete and final deliverance from sin and death, fulfilling the symbolism of the Passover lamb (1 Corinthians 5:7).

2. The Tabernacle and its Furnishings

Old Testament Type: The Tabernacle, described in Exodus 25-27, was a portable sanctuary where God's presence dwelled among His people. It included the Holy Place and the Most Holy Place, with items such as the altar, the table of showbread, and the golden lampstand. These elements were significant in the worship and approach to God.

New Testament Fulfillment: In the New Testament, Jesus fulfills the symbolic aspects of the Tabernacle. John 1:14 says, "The Word became flesh and made his dwelling among us," with "dwelling" meaning He "tabernacled" among us. Hebrews 9 explains that Jesus is the high priest who entered the true heavenly Tabernacle, offering His own blood for our redemption (Hebrews 9:11-12). The Old Testament Tabernacle's symbolism of God's presence and access to Him is realized in Christ, who provides a direct relationship with God.

3. The Bronze Serpent

Old Testament Type: In Numbers 21:4-9, the Israelites were bitten by venomous snakes as a result of their complaints against God. God instructed Moses to make a bronze serpent and lift it up on a pole. Those who looked at it were healed from the snake bites.

New Testament Fulfillment: Jesus refers to this event in John 3:14-15, saying, "Just as Moses lifted up the snake in the wilderness, so the Son of Man must be lifted up, that everyone who believes may have eternal life in him." The bronze serpent prefigures Jesus' crucifixion. Just as looking at the serpent brought physical healing, faith in Jesus' sacrificial death brings spiritual healing and eternal life.

4. The Manna in the Wilderness

Old Testament Type: During the Israelites' journey through the wilderness, God provided manna, a daily bread from heaven, as described in Exodus 16. This manna sustained the Israelites physically during their journey.

New Testament Fulfillment: In John 6:31-35, Jesus identifies Himself as the "bread of life," contrasting the manna with His own body, which provides eternal sustenance. He declares, "I am the bread of life. Whoever comes to me will never go hungry, and whoever believes in me will never be thirsty." Jesus fulfills the symbolism of manna by offering Himself as the true bread that satisfies spiritual hunger and provides eternal life.

5. The Sacrificial System

Old Testament Type: The Old Testament sacrificial system, detailed in Leviticus, involved various offerings and sacrifices to atone for sin and maintain a relationship with God. These included burnt offerings, sin offerings, and peace offerings.

New Testament Fulfillment: Jesus is portrayed as the ultimate sacrifice who fulfills the Old Testament sacrificial system. Hebrews 10:10-14 explains that Jesus' single, perfect sacrifice replaces the continual animal sacrifices of the Old Testament: "We have been made holy through the sacrifice of the body of Jesus Christ once for all." His sacrifice is sufficient to atone for sin and establish a new covenant (Hebrews 9:15).

6. The High Priest

Old Testament Type: The High Priest, as outlined in Leviticus, played a crucial role in mediating between God and the people, offering sacrifices and entering the Most Holy Place to atone for the sins of Israel.

New Testament Fulfillment: Jesus is depicted as the ultimate High Priest in Hebrews 4:14-16, who not only mediates but also offers Himself as the perfect sacrifice. His priesthood surpasses the Old Testament system, as He enters the heavenly sanctuary to intercede for believers and provides direct access to God (Hebrews 7:24-27).

These examples illustrate how the Old Testament types and shadows find their fulfillment in the New Testament through Jesus Christ. They reflect a profound continuity in God's plan for redemption, with Christ embodying and completing the symbols and promises of the old covenant. This shift from types and shadows to the reality of Christ enriches our understanding of the Old Testament and highlights the transformative impact of the New Covenant.

From Glory to Glory: The transition from Old Testament practices to New Testament fulfillment highlights a significant evolution in how God relates to His people. Two key practices in this transition are the Sabbath and circumcision. In the Old Testament, the Sabbath was a day of rest and worship observed on the seventh day, while circumcision was a crucial sign of the covenant between God and His people. With the advent of Jesus Christ, these practices were redefined and transformed, illustrating a deeper understanding of spiritual fulfillment and identity in the New Covenant.

Sabbath: Old Testament Significance vs. New Testament Fulfillment

In the Old Testament, the Sabbath was established as a fundamental aspect of God's covenant with Israel. As outlined in Exodus 20:8-11, it was a day set apart for rest and worship, reflecting God's rest after creation. The Sabbath was not merely a day off but a sacred time to reconnect with God, embodying a rhythm of work and rest that was central to Jewish identity and religious life.

However, the New Testament presents a redefined view of the Sabbath. Jesus Christ's arrival marked a shift from strict adherence to the Sabbath laws to a new understanding of spiritual rest. In Matthew 5:17, Jesus affirms that He did not come to abolish the law but to fulfill it. This fulfillment is further explained in Colossians 2:16-17, where Paul writes, "Therefore do not let anyone judge you by what you eat or drink, or regarding a religious festival, a New Moon celebration or a Sabbath day. These are a shadow of the things that were to come; the reality, however, is found in Christ." For Christians, the Sabbath is now seen through the lens of Christ's resurrection, celebrated on Sunday, which symbolizes the new creation and spiritual rest found in Him.

The Transition from the Old Testament Sabbath to the New Testament Lord's Day

The concept of the Sabbath represents one of the most profound shifts in religious observance from the Old Testament to the New Testament. Originally established on the seventh day of the week, the Sabbath was a day of rest and worship, deeply embedded in the fabric of Jewish life and identity. However, with the advent of Jesus Christ and the establishment of the New Testament church, this observance underwent a significant transformation. This transition is not merely a change in the day of rest but reflects deeper theological and practical shifts in how the early Christians understood their relationship with God and the nature of worship.

The Old Testament Sabbath

In the Old Testament, the Sabbath was instituted as the seventh day of the week, a day set aside for rest and reflection. As outlined in Exodus 20:8-11, this day was established by God as a covenantal sign between Him and Israel, commemorating His rest after the creation of the world. Observing the Sabbath involved abstaining from work and engaging in worship and spiritual renewal. This practice was deeply ingrained in Jewish culture and was seen as a critical aspect of maintaining a holy relationship with God. The Sabbath served as a weekly pause from the busyness of life, providing time to focus on God and refresh physically and spiritually.

The New Testament Shift

The New Testament introduces a significant shift from the traditional Sabbath observance. With the resurrection of Jesus Christ occurring on the first day of the week (Sunday), early Christians began to gather and celebrate this day as the Lord's Day, marking a new beginning for their weekly worship practices. This shift is highlighted in several New Testament passages:

- Acts 20:7: The early church gathered on the first day of the week to break bread and listen to Paul's teachings, indicating that Sunday became the primary day for Christian worship.

- 1 Corinthians 16:2: Paul instructs the believers to set aside their offerings on the first day of the week, further suggesting that Sunday was established as a day of gathering and worship.

This change reflects a deeper theological shift rather than a mere alteration of the day of rest. Jesus' resurrection on the first day of the week symbolizes the new creation and the fulfillment of the promises of the old covenant. The early Christians' decision to observe Sunday rather than the traditional Sabbath underscores the significance of Jesus' resurrection as the cornerstone of their faith.

Jesus and the Lord's Day

The New Testament emphasizes that Jesus redefines the concept of rest and worship. While the Old Testament Sabbath was a day of physical rest, Jesus' teachings and resurrection introduce a new dimension of spiritual rest and activity:

- **Matthew 5:17: Jesus states, "Do not think that I have come to abolish the Law or the Prophets; I have not come to abolish them but to fulfill them."** This fulfillment includes the reorientation of Sabbath observance to reflect the new covenant in Christ.

- **Mark 2:27: Jesus explains, "The Sabbath was made for man, not man for the Sabbath."** This teaching underscores that the purpose of the Sabbath is to serve humanity's need for rest and spiritual renewal rather than to impose a rigid legalistic framework.

In this context, the "Lord's Day" or Sunday becomes a celebration of the new creation and the resurrection, emphasizing joy and the new life offered in Christ. Rather than focusing on cessation from work, the early Christians embraced this day as a time to celebrate the victory over sin and death, marking a shift in how they experienced and expressed their faith.

Implications for Early Christians

For early Christians, the move from observing the Sabbath on the seventh day to worshiping on the first day of the week was more than a logistical change; it represented a profound theological shift. The resurrection of Jesus transformed the understanding of rest and worship, making Sunday a day of celebration and proclamation of the gospel rather than merely a day of physical rest. This new observance reflected the heart of Christian faith— living in the light of Christ's resurrection and sharing in the new life He offers.

The transition from the Old Testament Sabbath on the seventh day to the New Testament Lord's Day on the first day of the week highlights a significant development in religious practice and theology. Jesus' resurrection on Sunday redefined the meaning of rest and worship, shifting from a day of physical cessation to a celebration of spiritual renewal and new creation. This transformation underscores the fulfillment of Old Testament promises and the establishment of a new covenant in Christ, shaping the early Christian understanding of their faith and practice.

Any other examples?

Circumcision, as mandated in Genesis 17:10-14, was a critical sign of the covenant between God and Abraham's descendants. It marked a physical commitment to God's promises and was a defining feature of Jewish identity. Circumcision was a public declaration of one's inclusion in the covenant community.

The New Testament, however, introduces baptism as the new sign of covenant membership. In Colossians 2:11-12, Paul explains that in Christ, believers experience a "circumcision not performed by human hands" through baptism: "In him you were also circumcised, with a circumcision not performed by human hands. Your whole self ruled by the flesh was put off when you were circumcised by Christ, having been buried with him in baptism, in which you were also raised with him through your faith in the working of God, who raised him from the dead." Baptism symbolizes the inward transformation and spiritual rebirth that circumcision once represented, marking a believer's entry into the New Covenant and their identification with Christ's death and resurrection.

Theological Shift: Old vs. New Covenant Perspectives

In the Old Testament, both the Sabbath and circumcision were crucial for maintaining covenantal identity and obedience. They were tangible signs of God's promises and His people's commitment to Him. The Sabbath served as a reminder of God's creation and His provision, while circumcision was a mark of belonging to God's chosen people.

With the New Testament, the focus shifts from these physical practices to the spiritual realities fulfilled in Christ. The Sabbath, while still acknowledged, is now understood as fulfilled in the resurrection, shifting the focus to Sunday as a celebration of new life in Christ. Circumcision, once a physical mark of covenant membership, is replaced by baptism, symbolizing the spiritual transformation and new identity offered through Jesus.

The transition from the Old Testament practices of the Sabbath and circumcision to their New Testament fulfillments reflects a profound shift in divine-human relations. These changes underscore the transformative impact of Christ's work, moving from physical observances to spiritual realities. The Sabbath is fulfilled in the new creation celebrated on Sunday, and circumcision is replaced by baptism, marking a new era of spiritual renewal and covenantal identity. This evolution highlights the depth and breadth of Christ's redemptive work, fulfilling and transcending the old covenant with a new understanding of faith and relationship with God.

So, What's the Point?

In essence, the Sabbath is transformed from a day of mere rule-following to a symbol of spiritual rest in Christ. It's about blending the old with the new, honoring the rich history while embracing the deeper spiritual meaning that Jesus offers.

The Sabbath, whether viewed through a theological, historical, or practical lens, remains a profound and transformative practice. In today's fast-paced world, it stands as a countercultural declaration, challenging the relentless grind of productivity and the pervasive "always-on" mindset. Observing the Sabbath—regardless of the specific day chosen—conveys a powerful message to society: the necessity of rest, reflection, and reconnection is not only a divine mandate but also a critical human need. It transcends theology, serving as a reminder that pausing to restore our minds, bodies, and spirits is essential for leading a balanced, meaningful life.

At its core, the Sabbath is about so much more than mere rule-following or religious obligation. It invites us to dwell in a space where time is sacred, relationships are deepened, and our inner lives are prioritized. In honoring the Sabbath, we reclaim our right to exist beyond productivity, reminding ourselves and others that there is more to life than constant striving. This ancient tradition, grounded in both divine intention and human need, speaks to the universal longing for peace, balance, and purpose.

Ultimately, the Sabbath is not just a relic of the past or a theological debate; it's a timeless practice that holds extraordinary relevance today. It teaches us to respect the natural rhythm of work and rest, urging us to step back, breathe, and reconnect—with ourselves, with others, and with the divine. As we rediscover the Sabbath's true meaning, we find a path to deeper fulfillment, offering not only spiritual nourishment but also a much-needed remedy for the modern soul. Whether viewed through the lens of faith or as an essential part of mental and emotional well-being, keeping the Sabbath reminds us of all that rest is a gift we cannot afford to ignore.

So how should

Christian's Sabbath?

Given the deep connection between Jesus and the Sabbath, Christians can approach the Sabbath in a way that honors both its original purpose and its fulfillment in Christ. Here's how Christians might consider approaching the Sabbath:

1. *Embrace Rest, Not Legalism*

The Sabbath, as Jesus emphasized, was made for humanity's benefit (Mark 2:27). Rather than approaching it as a rigid set of rules, Christians can view the Sabbath as a gift of rest and renewal. It's about intentionally stepping away from the demands of work and busyness to focus on spiritual health and well-being.

2. *Seek Spiritual Renewal in Christ*

Since Jesus offers ultimate spiritual rest (Matthew 11:28), the Sabbath is a time to draw near to Him. Christians can use this day for prayer, Bible study, worship, and reflection on God's presence and provision. It's a day to renew and deepen one's relationship with Christ, who embodies the true meaning of rest.

3. *Do Good and Serve Others*

Jesus demonstrated that the Sabbath is not just about resting but also about doing good (Mark 3:1-6). Christians can approach the Sabbath with a heart for service, finding ways to help others, care for those in need, and show kindness. The Sabbath should be a time for both personal renewal and acts of compassion.

4. *Reflect on Creation and Redemption*

The original Sabbath was rooted in God's rest after creation (Genesis 2:2-3), while the new understanding of Sabbath in Christ is tied to redemption and resurrection. Christians can use the Sabbath to reflect on God's work in creation and salvation, thanking God for the beauty of the world and the redemption they have in Jesus.

5. *Celebrate Jesus' Resurrection*

Many Christians observe Sunday, the "Lord's Day," as their Sabbath because it commemorates Jesus' resurrection (Acts 20:7). The resurrection is central to Christian faith, so the Sabbath can be a joyful celebration of Jesus' victory over death and the new life He brings.

6. *Practice Balance and Well-being*

In the fast-paced modern world, the Sabbath is an opportunity to practice balance, rest, and mental health. Christians can use the day to recharge emotionally, physically, and spiritually. It's not just a break from work but a conscious effort to prioritize what matters most: faith, family, community, and well-being.

Conclusion

For Christians, the Sabbath should be a day that reflects the rest, renewal, and freedom found in Christ. It's not about legalistic restrictions but about experiencing God's grace, doing good, and enjoying the fullness of life that Jesus offers. By observing the Sabbath in this way, Christians can find deeper spiritual meaning and connection to God, while honoring the rich biblical tradition of rest.

References

- Holy Bible, New International Version (NIV)

- Brueggemann, Walter. *Sabbath as Resistance: Saying No to the Culture of Now*. Westminster John Knox Press, 2014.

- Heschel, Abraham Joshua. *The Sabbath: Its Meaning for Modern Man*. Farrar, Straus and Giroux, 2005.

Council of Laodicea, Canon 29. (363-364 AD). The Apostolic Fathers: Volume II, Epistle of Barnabas. Epistle to the Smyrneans. Epistle to Diognetus. Translated by Bart D. Ehrman. Harvard University Press, 2003.

Catechism of the Catholic Church, Paragraph 2175.

Catechism of the Catholic Church. Vatican

Publishing House, 1994. Online Access

Pope John Paul II, Dies Domini. (1998). Vatican

Press. Online Access

Genesis 2:2-3. The Holy Bible, New International

Version (NIV). Biblica, 2011.

Exodus 20:8-11. The Holy Bible, New International

Version (NIV). Biblica, 2011.

Acts 20:7. The Holy Bible, New International Version

(NIV). Biblica, 2011.

1 Corinthians 16:2. The Holy Bible, New

International Version (NIV). Biblica, 2011.

Emperor Constantine's Edict of 321 AD. The

Apostolic Fathers: Volume I, I Clement. II Clement.

Ignatius. Polycarp. Translated by Bart D. Ehrman.

Harvard University Press, 2003.+

Made in the USA
Columbia, SC
01 October 2024

42759674R00078